SMALL GROUP MEMBER DISCUSSION GUIDE

SOUL CRAVING

❧ AN INVITATION TO THE FEAST THAT SATISFIES ❧

A 6-SESSION BIBLE STUDY

BY JOEL WARNE

Standard®
PUBLISHING
Bringing The Word to Life
Cincinnati, Ohio

Published by Standard Publishing, Cincinnati, Ohio
www.standardpub.com

Soul Craving, ISBN 978-0-7847-1955-8, text © Joel Warne

Written by: Joel Warne
Visit the author's website, www.WellspringLifeResources.com

Project Editor: Michael Mack and Margaret Williams

Cover and interior design: Mattson Creative

ISBN: 978-0-7847-1993-4

13   12   11   10   09   08   07   9   8   7   6   5   4   3   2   1

Contents

Leader Guide

If you are reading this page, it probably means that part of your personal journey with Jesus Christ includes walking alongside others on theirs. Yet, as a *Soul Craving* group leader, your first job is . . . to give up!

Why? Because you cannot create spiritual fullness in your group members—and God doesn't expect you to try. The *Soul Craving* leader's main role is simply to encourage group members to notice the ways they are hungry for God and to point them to his rich banquet table. Isn't that a relief? That means you don't need to know more than anybody else in your group. You only need to know the one to whom to direct their hungry lives.

The thoughts below offer helpful suggestions to you as leader of your *Soul Craving* group or class. So relax, pull up a chair, and enjoy the feast!

VALUES

Soul Craving classes and groups are fed by three key values:

GRACE—In discipleship programs in recent years, the word *accountability* has become big: accountability to attend, to pray, to stay clear of certain taboo behaviors, to serve, to witness—to do "the stuff." *Soul Craving* groups understand accountability differently. We hold one another accountable first and foremost to live by grace. In this way of living, our behaviors spring from something deeper—a warm, responsive, and ultimately transforming relationship with God. *Soul Craving* groups and classes call us to live as God's beloved children in a relationship of grace, listening, and personal responsiveness to the Holy Spirit. This is the special banquet of the soul at which we are privileged guests.

LISTENING—*Soul Craving* groups revolve around listening to God and each other. As we share around the Scripture passages and readings, we practice a listening, worshipful heart—a heart that is respectfully in tune with what God is doing in each of us. This group is not about "fixing" people. Few actions close the Holy Spirit out of the process like a group member or leader intent on fixing another member whose opinion differs from theirs or who is perhaps in need of God's touch. We are not one another's saviors, but fellow travelers who humbly, lovingly, and respectfully travel together, pointing each other to our ultimate guide, Jesus Christ.

Worship—Worship is fundamental to feeding our souls in Christ. The heart of the worshiper tends to be open, soft, vulnerable, and attentive—all characteristics needed for a growing awareness of God's nourishing presence in our lives. Much emphasis is given during group sessions to inviting an atmosphere in which worshipful hearts connect with God.

COMPONENTS

The *Soul Craving* study includes the following components:

<u>BEFORE SESSIONS</u>

Soul Craving at-home readings and associated Bible reflections
> —*To allow each member personal time with God to become aware of God's invitation to greater intimacy*

<u>DURING SESSIONS</u>

Devotional Open
> —*To make room for a listening, worshipful atmosphere for the meeting*

Discussion of the *Soul Craving* reading and Bible reflections
> —*To clarify and help process one or two specific things God may be offering each member through the book and Bible reflections*

Tip: Always guide the discussions toward practical, real, and self-revealing conversation rather than simply theoretical talk. Encourage participants to share how the material connects with the real hopes and desires, worries and fears, discouragements or predicaments they are currently experiencing. The group members will largely follow the level of authenticity you model. When you risk being real, it gives the group permission to do likewise.

Big Tip: "What people really need is a good listening to!"

—Mary Lou Casey

As a leader and participant, your greatest gift to the other group members is not your input but your ears! Creating a prayerful and safe environment allows the transparency needed to open transforming doorways between our hearts and God's Spirit.

Group Bible Reflection

—To experience God together in a reflection that is thematically connected with the session topic

Tip: The emphasis of the group Bible meditation time is not to exhaustively study the passage, but to encourage the group members to become aware of one or two words, phrases, or ideas that the Holy Spirit may want to make alive in their lives today. Questions that reflect the intent of this time might include:

What single new thing do I sense God inviting me toward through this passage?

What power, comfort, conviction, or inspiration is God offering my life through its words?

This approach to Scripture underlines, once again, the intention of the *Soul Craving* study: to encourage a life of worshipful listening, celebration, and responsiveness to God.

Closing Prayer

—To recall, clarify, and plant God's personal word in each member

Tip: Because of its importance in anchoring God's Word deeply in the members' lives, carefully protect this closing prayer time!

AFTER SESSIONS

Take-Away Activity

—To give members one or two practical ways to weave the truths of the session into their lives between group meetings

DESTINATION

In the *Soul Craving* sessions, we are not as intent on gaining new information about God as we are in pausing to absorb the impact of things we have perhaps known for a long time: God's love for us, his desire to share this love in the midst of our ordinary daily activities, his ability to relieve us of the God-substitutes we use to get through life, his longing to show us the reality of his unique plan for us, and much more. Worship and listening. Hearing, digesting, and responding. This is what our souls crave. This is where we're going.

Blessings as you richly feast in Christ!

HUNGRY

"LONGING, PAIN, ANXIETIES, AND OTHER INSISTENT AND NAMELESS YEARNINGS ARE ALL SIGNALS THAT MY SOUL CRAVES TO BE FED. THE CHALLENGE, IN A WORLD IN WHICH WE ARE SURROUNDED BY JUNK FOOD FOR THE SOUL, IS TO CULTIVATE A HABIT OF FEEDING UPON JESUS CHRIST, THE HEAVENLY BANQUET."

SOUL CRAVING, PP. 29, 30

SAMPLING THE FEAST
Preparing for the Group Session

Complete the following at home:
♦ Read chapters 1–3 in *Soul Craving*
♦ Ponder the Bible reflections on page 12
♦ Jot down some thoughts in response to questions 1–3

1. Note one or two ideas that especially get your attention in the chapter readings and At-Home Bible Reflections for this session.

Feasting

Lovers.

"Slaves"?

> LEADER PREPARATION
> In addition to the preparation on this page:
> ♦ read this lesson beforehand, noting ideas that seem important for the discussion
> ♦ prepare paper slips for the *Group Bible Reflection*
> ♦ review the Leader's Guide at the beginning of this guide for a successful group
> ♦ pray for the group members

2. If you could distill to just one word what God is speaking to you as you reflect on the material, what would that word be? Why does this word emerge for you?

time - feasting takes time - its nourishment, celebration, fellowship, relational

3. What is one practical way you will respond this week to God's call to you through the Bible reflections and readings? (Additional journaling pages 44–48.)

AT-HOME BIBLE REFLECTIONS

Use these optional Bible Reflections to add a deep richness to the group experience.

Reflection 1
Matthew 13:44-46

These brief verses emphasize the precious, often hidden treasure that is our relationship with God. Ponder where God may be hidden in your world right now—at home, at work, in your relationships, joys, struggles, or pain. What habits or postures of the heart would help you be more aware of his presence? Like the people in the passage, what might you need to trade to possess God more fully? Jot your thoughts below or in a separate journal.

It is the "one thing" of great value

I may need to trade my own agenda

During these reflections, if a certain word or phrase from the passage especially speaks to you, stay with it, listening to God and interacting with him. Feel free to leave the rest of the passage for another time.

Reflection 2
Isaiah 55:1-3

Isaiah offers us a gift in these words. According to the passage, the food and drink needed to meet our deepest human hungers and thirsts are free for the asking. Read the passage several times, pausing to absorb any word, phrase, or idea that emerges. Express to God the longings or worship stirred by the passage. Write down your impressions.

Come come come   Listen listen

Possible ways to interact with this passage:

Verse 1:   Feed your soul on Jesus as your "wine and milk."

Verse 2:   Notice ways you tend to spend yourself on "what does not satisfy." What would it look like to delight your soul in rich fare instead?

Verse 3:   Spend some time quietly noticing any counsel or encouragement God has been speaking to you lately "that your soul may live."

TOGETHER AT THE TABLE
Group Session

♦   Encourage a moment of worshipful quiet before the opening readings.

♦   If the group size is more than ten, consider breaking into subgroups of four to discuss the reading and At-Home Bible Reflections. Come together in the full group for the *Group Bible Reflection*. Notice what subgroup arrangement works best for your group.

Devotional Open

Open the group session by reading aloud the following quote. Invite a minute or two of response.

"Hearts that are 'fit to break' with love for the Godhead are those who have been in the Presence and have looked with opened eye upon the majesty of Deity. . . . To penetrate, to push in sensitive living experience into the holy Presence, is a privilege open to every child of God."

A. W. Tozer

Read the passage below followed by an opening prayer asking God to be central and honored in the group today.

"Come, all you who are thirsty, come to the waters; and you who have no money, come, buy and eat! Come, buy wine and milk without money and without cost. Why spend money on what is not bread, and your labor on what does not satisfy? Listen, listen to me, and eat what is good, and your soul will delight in the richest of fare. Give ear and come to me; hear me, that your soul may live" (Isaiah 55:1-3).

Review the At-Home Prep

Prepare for the discussion by spending a minute glancing through the thoughts you noted at home about Questions 1–3 on page 8.

Discussion

Begin the discussion by sharing your response to question 1 on page 8, prepared at home before the session.

When ready, continue your discussion by responding to the following quotes from *Soul Craving*.

PAST PERFECT

"I am a pretty good example of the religious-duties-as-faith approach to God. Growing up, I somehow picked up the idea that although God loved me, he didn't like me very much. He loved me because he was God. It was his job to love me. But to get him to like me required that I perform for

him at a constantly high level. That sort of relationship with God—one of endless vigilance to keep our accounts current through correct behavior, right thinking, and religious work—deserves to be shrunk to as narrow a sliver of life as possible. There is no water down that well."

Soul Craving, p. 18

Does the quote above connect in any way to your own experience of God? If so, what do you suppose causes this sort of religion?

HEART TO HEART

"But what if faith is something different? What if faith means a transforming relationship with someone who consistently breathes life and meaning into everything he touches? What if faith is a heart-to-heart relationship with someone who knows me deeply, accepts me totally, and has the power to increasingly restore my fragmented soul? What if faith opens a doorway into the personal reality every human soul has craved since the day we were born? That would be the sort of faith you would not want to limit, isolate, or confine to out-of-the-way areas of life. Instead, you would want that faith to overflow the few narrow streams of your heart through which it currently trickles until it floods your whole being."

Soul Craving, p. 19

Which of the following best describes your own relationship with God?
- ❏ religious employee
- ❏ friend
- ❏ child
- ❏ slave
- ❏ lover
- ❏ other: _____

If you have noticed movement in yourself toward the kind of relationship with God you most desire, what seems to have been a key in your transition?

When ready, discuss question 2 on page 8.

GROUP BIBLE REFLECTION
LUKE 15:11-32—A CHILD COMES HOME

Draw a slip of paper from the container on which is written the name of one character from the passage. A group member reads the passage aloud. Then spend about five minutes silently pondering the story from the perspective of the character you chose, jotting your thoughts in response to the following:

> Before the session, prepare slips of paper equal to the number of participants. On each slip write the name of one character from the *Group Bible Reflection* passage: Father, Elder Son, or Younger Son. Fold and place in a container ready for the session.

What hopes, needs or fears does this character experience in this story? What is God offering the character? How does he respond?

What is God speaking to me through this character or the passage in general? How does this connect with what I'm experiencing in life right now?

Discussion

After the time of silent reflection above, share your responses with the group.

Toward the end of your discussion, share your answers to question 3 on page 8, prepared at home.

Closing Prayer

Allow the group leader to guide you in this closing prayer.

Leader:

As you prayerfully think back over our time today, is there one thought or idea that stands out as most important? Might this be God speaking to you? Spend a moment prayerfully reflecting on this. (pause)

If something has especially spoken to you today, what would you like to say to God about this? Silently share your heart with God for a moment. (pause)

What, perhaps, would God like to say to you in return? (pause)

Finally, just relax in God's love and care for you. Invite God to plant his powerful Word deep inside you to grow and bear fruit in the days ahead. (pause)

Amen.

Take-Away Menu
15-Second Take-Away Activity

FOR THE LEADER
Consider creating a list of member e-mail addresses for use in sharing prayer concerns and communications in-between the group sessions.

LISTENING FOR GOD IN THE ORDINARY
A key goal of Christian faith is to dissolve the false distinction between "spiritual" activities and "regular" activities. It is not enough to simply spend more time doing "spiritual" things, but to allow every area of life to be an arena in which God's Spirit is given free sway. The brief 10–15 second exercise below may be woven through your ordinary, day-to-day activities this week to increase an experience of God's loving presence in all things.

Activity: From time to time, during an ordinary activity (making the bed, driving to work, watching the kids at the park, paying bills, sitting in traffic, walking to the mailbox, attending a business meeting, etc.), spend a moment intentionally listening for God's presence and movement in the thing that you are doing. Cock your inner ear to God. Ask:

♦   Lord, how are you present in this situation—right here, right now?
♦   Lord, how are you loving and delighting in me at this moment?

Note: It is quite possible that you may "hear" nothing special. Yet through this regular listening, this paying attention, you will gradually become more in tune with God's loving presence, movement, and calling in the ordinary activities of your life in the days ahead.

SAVORING HIS WORDS

"WHILE THE BIBLE CONTAINS WONDERFUL INFORMATION ABOUT GOD,
OUR GOAL IS NOT SIMPLY TO COLLECT IT, SORT IT, CATEGORIZE IT—
CONQUER IT. OUR GOAL IS TO CONSUME THE WORDS OF THE BIBLE AS
FOOD FOR OUR HUNGRY SOULS."

SOUL CRAVING, P. 60

SAMPLING THE FEAST
Preparing for the Group Session

Complete the following at home:
♦ Read chapters 4–6 in *Soul Craving*
♦ Ponder the Bible reflections on page 15
♦ Jot down some thoughts in response to
  questions 1–3

LEADER PREPARATION
In addition to the
preparation on this page:
♦ release the session to
  God, remembering
  that he is the group's
  teacher and leader
♦ read this lesson
  beforehand, noting
  ideas that seem
  important for the
  discussion
♦ prepare paper slips
  for the *Group Bible
  Reflection*
♦ pray for the group
  members

1. Note one or two ideas that especially get
your attention in the chapter readings and
At-Home Bible Reflections for this session.

Liberty Encourages unseen

Desperation   Digestion MW
Story of Bill. Ignore my Ficher in God - Stale food.
Word of God - living + active Heb 4:12

2. If you could distill to just one word what God is speaking to you as you
reflect on the material, what would that word be? Why does this word emerge
for you?

Desperation

3. What is one practical way you will respond this week to God's call to you
through the Bible reflections and readings?

Such a more meaningful time in scripture

AT-HOME BIBLE REFLECTIONS

Use these optional Bible Reflections to add a deep richness to the group experience.

Reflection 1
Mark 5:24-34
Using the "Read, Reflect, Respond, React" Bible meditation method described at the end of chapter 4 of *Soul Craving*, put yourself in the scene with the characters. Identify especially with the ill woman. Imagine yourself in her position. What was she feeling? What motivated her actions? Is there any way her need and experience are like yours right now? How might you touch the hem of Jesus' garment today? Note any impressions.

She was very tired
Feeling outcast
She had faith born of desperation
She felt the healing happen.
She was 5 options I had been used/abused.
Great peace of release new life

Consider spending a second session reflecting on Jesus in this passage. What do the availability and power he demonstrates in the passage offer you today?

He is all powerful - He wants to know me - He wants me to come to Him - He knows when we access Him

Reflection 2
Mark 1:40-42
Today use the slightly different method of Bible reflection described at the end of chapter 5, "Encounter." Allow the scene to gradually open itself up to you. What is the leper thinking, feeling, hoping for, or fearing? In what ways is his story like yours? During this or a second session, also consider the account through Jesus' eyes. What possibilities do his attitude toward the leper open up for your life?

He was desperate
He was humbled
He was willing to lay everything down before God.
He left it open for God to work.
He was sure of what God could do

During the final phase of the reflection, "Rest," allow yourself to sit quietly with God, unconcerned for a time about lingering needs or questions. Simply enjoy God and allow God to enjoy you.

Jesus loved Him

Was filled with compassion

Jesus reached out to him the leper

Jesus spoke and it was done

15

TOGETHER AT THE TABLE
Group Session

♦ Encourage a moment of worshipful quiet before the opening readings.

♦ If the group size is more than ten, consider breaking into subgroups of four to discuss the reading and At-Home Bible Reflections. Come together in the full group for the *Group Bible Reflection*. Notice what subgroup arrangement works best for your group.

Devotional Open

Open the group session by reading aloud the following quote. Invite a minute or two of response.

"The nature of water is soft, and that of stone is hard; but if a bottle is hung above the stone, allowing the water to fall down drop by drop, it wears away the stone. So it is with the Word of God: it is soft and our heart is hard, but the man [one] who hears the Word of God often opens his heart to the fear of God."

Abba Poemen

Read the passage below followed by an opening prayer asking God to be central and honored in the group today.

"My soul finds rest in God alone; my salvation comes from him. He alone is my rock and my salvation; he is my fortress, I will never be shaken. . . . Trust in him at all times, O people; pour out your hearts to him, for God is our refuge"
(Psalm 62:1, 2, 8).

Review the At-Home Prep

Prepare for the discussion by spending a minute glancing through the thoughts you noted at home about Questions 1–3 on page 14.

Discussion

Begin the discussion by sharing your response to question 1 on page 14, prepared at home before the session.

When ready, continue your discussion by responding to the following quotes from *Soul Craving*.

THE SAVOR OF SCRIPTURE

"Imagine an orchard at harvesttime. Imagine how puzzling it would be if, after working hard to gather in the fruit, the harvest crew simply left it crated on the ground to rot and moved on to the next orchard, there to do the same. Wouldn't that be strange? Moving from tree to tree, working hard, collecting fruit. Sorting, sizing, boxing, and stacking but leaving it all behind at the end of the day. Yet that is what we do with the Scriptures when we mentally harvest information from a passage yet move on before giving our spirits time to taste, chew, swallow, and digest its fruit."

Soul Craving, p. 60

[handwritten annotations: Digestion → mouth - taste, throat - swallow, stomach - broken down, sm. intest - absorbs nutrients, lg intestine nutrients gained, waste carried away, gas, constip.]

What do you long to experience with God during Bible reading? Can the "tasting and chewing" approach described at the end of chapters 4 and 5 of *Soul Craving* help you? What appeals to you about this method? What seems challenging?

FOGGY WEATHER

"Bible reading generates all sorts of unexpected reactions. Peculiar bouts of sleepiness, daydreams, pressing reminders of errands that need attention, a sense of having fallen inside a vast, spiritual fog. The Scriptures, taken in hand by any ordinary reader, have these effects and many others. Puzzling. Embarrassing. Galling!"

Soul Craving, p. 69

What Bible reading difficulty do you most struggle with right now? Do any of the highlighted tips in chapter 6, "Unstuck," speak to your problem? If so, how?

When ready, discuss question 2 on page 14.

GROUP BIBLE REFLECTION
MARK 10:46-52—A NEEDY MAN CRIES OUT

A group member reads the passage aloud. Using the "Read, Reflect, Respond, React" Bible meditation method outlined below, spend 5–7 minutes silently pondering the story.

Note: Remember, it's natural to sometimes receive nothing especially personal from a passage of Scripture. Sometimes a text speaks to us now; at other times we receive it as a seed that grows and produces fruit later.

During the *Group Bible Reflection* sharing, either go around the circle to give everyone a chance to speak or simply ask those who want to share to do so. If the discussion becomes too theoretical, gently guide the focus back to God's personal word to each member through the text.

READ: Read the passage a few times to get the big picture. What is the main message of the text?

REFLECT: What single word, phrase, or impression especially whispers to you from the passage? Might the Holy Spirit be speaking something to you through this?

Mentally picture one or more characters. What are their thoughts, fears, or desires? What risks do they take or avoid? How does God respond? How is your story like theirs?

RESPOND: Express any thoughts, longings, or worship the passage inspires.

REACT: How will you live the truth of this passage in the days ahead?

Discussion
After the time of silent reflection above, share your responses with the group.

Toward the end of your discussion, share your answers to question 3 on page 14, prepared at home.

Closing Prayer

Allow the group leader to guide you in this closing prayer.

Leader:

As you prayerfully think back over our time today, what is the one thought or idea that stands out as most important to you? Might this be God speaking to you? Spend a moment prayerfully reflecting on this. (pause)

If something has especially spoken to you today, what would you like to say to God about this? Silently share your heart with God for a moment. (pause)

What, perhaps, would God like to say to you in return? (pause)

Finally, just relax in God's love and care for you. Invite God to plant his powerful Word deep inside you to grow and bear fruit in the days ahead. (pause)

Amen.

Take-Away Menu
10-Second Take-Away Activity

PICTURES OF TRANSFORMATION

Activity: When reading books of the Bible that tell historical accounts (the Gospels, Acts, Old Testament historical books, etc.), identify one moment in the story that especially speaks to you. Use your imagination to capture a mental "snapshot" of that moment. Later, during your ordinary daily activites, return from time to time for a few seconds to that mental picture, allowing its truths to encourage, comfort, and call you back to your real self in Christ.

SESSION THREE

The Flavor of Intimacy

"Worship seeks God. Worship yearns, leans, cranes, listens for a commander. There is a throne at the center of the universe from which God reigns. Worship longingly feels its way there."

Soul Craving, p. 118

Sampling the Feast
Preparing for the Group Session

Complete the following at home:
♦ Read chapters 7–9 in *Soul Craving*
♦ Ponder the Bible reflections on next page
♦ Jot down some thoughts in response to questions 1–3

1. Note one or two ideas that especially get your attention in the chapter readings and At-Home Bible Reflections for this session.

Leader Preparation
In addition to the preparation on this page:
♦ read this lesson before-hand, noting ideas that seem important for the discussion
♦ prepare paper slips for the *Group Bible Reflection*
♦ review the suggestions at the beginning of this guide for a successful group
♦ pray for the group members

2. If you could distill to just one word what God is speaking to you as you reflect on the material, what would that word be? Why does this word emerge for you?

3. What is one practical way you will respond this week to God's call to you through the Bible reflections and readings?

At-Home Bible Reflections

Reflection 1
2 Kings 20:1-6
Using the Bible meditation methods you learned in earlier lessons, form a mental picture of this scene. Like Hezekiah, is there any area of your life that feels "ill" and "at the point of death" (v. 1)? What situation or concern makes you want to turn to the wall and weep bitterly to God? Transparently invite God into the pain, needs, and longings that you have been keeping only to yourself. Write your prayer below or in a separate journal.

Reflection 2
John 21:1-14
Using this passage as a springboard for worship, meditate on a few verses at a time, allowing your mind and heart to move between mental reflection and inner listening.

Some ways to respond to the passage include:

Verses 1-3   How do you feel when laboring hard without Christ?
Verses 4-7   Respond to Jesus' invitation to be at his side.
Verses 8, 9   Enjoy the feast Jesus has prepared for you.
Verses 10, 11   Receive Jesus' call to service.
Verses 12, 13   Rest, feed, be full in Christ.

Together at the Table

Group Session

For the Leader

Notice those in the group who have not had a chance to share in the previous sessions. Give them an opportunity to do so during the discussion time today, respecting the choice of some to decline.

Devotional Open

Open the group session by reading aloud the following quote. Invite a minute or two of response.

"Prayer and helplessness are inseparable. Only he who is helpless can truly pray. . . . Your infant child cannot formulate in words a single petition to you. Yet the little one prays the best way he knows how. All he can do is to cry, but you understand very well his pleading."

O. Hallesby

Read the passage below followed by an opening prayer asking God to be central and honored in the group today.

"My soul yearns, even faints, for the courts of the Lord; my heart and my flesh cry out for the living God. . . . Better is one day in your courts than a thousand elsewhere; I would rather be a doorkeeper in the house of my God than dwell in the tents of the wicked" (Psalm 84:2,10).

Review the At-Home Prep

Prepare for the discussion by spending a minute glancing through the thoughts you noted at home about Questions 1–3 on page 20.

Discussion

Begin the discussion by sharing your response to question 1 on page 20, prepared at home before the session.

When ready, continue your discussion by responding to the following quotes from *Soul Craving*.

SEE-THROUGH HEART

"God's intense desire to be near us, to share in those things that distress us most, leads him to knock at the door of our unresolved messes—our confusions and weaknesses, our sinful habits and lingering pains. Paradoxically, the way forward into new life in Christ is to invite him into the remains of our old life. There he comforts and kills, consoles and consumes, destroys and re-creates. A see-through heart is one short step away from a re-created heart."

Soul Craving, p. 86

How do you relate to God concerning the failures and "messes" in your life? Must you hide them? work intensely to clean them up? What would happen instead if you simply relaxed transparently and lovingly with God in them? Have you ever done this? What was the result?

WORSHIP IGNITES CONTACT

"Some have said that Paul would have been a great preacher to listen to on Sunday but a real pain to be around on Monday. Why? Because he was so focused on Christ that he never let up. He never turned it off. While I think the evidence shows that Paul may have been a little more diplomatic than that, you can see the point. Paul was intense. He had seen something; he had been there. He had made contact; he was a changed man. This is the effect of that personal vision of God experienced in worship."

Soul Craving, p. 126

For you, what is the connection between worship and a growing vision of Christ in your life? What small gods would need to die for Jesus to grow larger in your eyes? What effect might this have for how you experience life?

When ready, discuss question 2 on page 20.

GROUP BIBLE REFLECTION
LUKE 7:36-50—A SORROWING HEART

Before the session, prepare slips of paper equal to the number of participants. On each slip write the name of one character from the *Group Bible Reflection* passage: Jesus, Woman, Pharisee, or Guests. Fold and place in a container ready for the session.

Select a slip of paper on which is written the name of one character from the passage. A group member reads the passage aloud. Then spend about five minutes silently pondering the story from the perspective of the character you chose, jotting your thoughts in response to the following: What part does transparency with God play in the passage? How does this character respond? What hopes, needs, or fears does he or she experience?

What is God speaking to me through this character or the passage in general? What does this offer for my life right now?

Discussion
After the time of silent reflection above, share your responses with the group.

Toward the end of your discussion, share your answers to question 3 on page 20, prepared at home.

Closing Prayer
Allow the group leader to guide you in this closing prayer.

> **Leader:**
> *As you prayerfully think back over our time today, what is one thought or idea that stands out as most important to you? Might this be God speaking to you? Spend a moment prayerfully reflecting on this. (pause)*
>
> *If something has especially spoken to you today, what would you like to say to God about this? Silently share your heart with God for a moment. (pause)*
>
> *What, perhaps, would God like to say to you in return? (pause)*

Finally, just relax in God's love and care for you. Invite God to plant his powerful Word deep inside you to grow and bear fruit in the days ahead. (pause)

Amen.

Take-Away Menu
2–3 Minute Take-Away Activity

LISTENING FOR GOD'S NEW THING
God is always ready to birth new, liberating things in your world—pivotal things that at this moment do not enter your imagination but which you need. There is a kind of attentive listening that invites God's new thing to begin to stir in you.

Activity: Spend 2–3 minutes a day sitting quietly before God, giving him loving permission to speak to your deep places. It is not necessary that you feel anything in particular, only that you consciously invite Jesus Christ to be active in birthing new things in you. You may want to speak an invitation aloud to God or write it down, signing your name:

> *Dear Lord, beyond those areas that get my focus and energy, what else are you poised to do in my life? What new thing would you like to make alive in my outlook, relationships, career, ministry, or other areas? I'm here and available, Lord. Speak, your servant is listening.*

As you pray like this over the days ahead, some surprising activity of God's choosing will likely begin to percolate in you.

Note: Physical actions and symbols can sometimes help anchor and express our prayers.

- As you listen for God's new thing, rest open, asking hands on your lap.
- Place an empty bowl next to your prayer space representing your life as an open, available vessel. Touch the bowl prayerfully from time to time while praying and even during the day.
- Draw a picture of your life as a waiting canvas and offer it to the Lord.

RELISHING HIS PURPOSE

"ON BEING AWAKENED BY GOD, THE QUESTION BECOMES 'WHAT ARE MY
PRESENT RELATIONSHIPS ABOUT?' WHILE BEFORE, THE PEOPLE IN MY LIFE
SEEMED THERE TO FURTHER MY INTERESTS, TO SERVE ME OR ENTERTAIN ME,
NOW I SEE MYSELF AS THE SERVANT OF GOD'S GRACE GROWING IN THEM."

SOUL CRAVING, P. 145

SAMPLING THE FEAST
Preparing for the Group Session

Complete the following at home:
♦ Read chapters 10–12 in *Soul Craving*
♦ Ponder the Bible reflections on the next page
♦ Jot down some thoughts in response to
   questions 1–3

1. Note one or two ideas that especially get
your attention in the chapter readings and
At-Home Bible Reflections for this session.

> Purpose - Gods priority list · ours?
> Calling · Islands of light
> Self Discovery· Natural Strengths, Passions, Spiritual Gifts

2. If you could distill to just one word what God is speaking to you as you
reflect on the material, what would that word be? Why does this word emerge
for you?

> the whole money thing - a better steward
> ask God believing

3. What is one practical way you will respond this week to God's call to you
through the Bible reflections and readings?

LEADER PREPARATION
In addition to the preparation on this page:
♦ during the session, continually release the meeting to God, knowing he is present and active
♦ read this lesson beforehand, noting ideas that seem important for the discussion
♦ pray for the group members

At-Home Bible Reflections

Reflection
The Scripture reflections for this session are combined into a single, longer reflection. If time allows, ponder the passages over several days. On the lines next to the references, write two or three key words that capture the essence of the passage.

SCRIPTURE	KEY WORDS
Matthew 5:14-16	light ; lifted up.
1 Peter 4:10, 11	Words of God, strength of God, God's grace, God praised
2 Corinthians 5:17-20	reconciliation
Mark 9:33-35	upside down greatest - servant first must be last
Matthew 22:35-40	Love.

Drawing from the key words above, create a single sentence that summarizes God's core purpose for his children in this world.

Lift up your light being grounded in God, speak the ministry of reconciliation and this upside down kingdom involved in love.

What feelings emerge as you ponder such a purpose for yourself? Listen to both your positive and negative responses. Does God's purpose stir in you new directions or possibilities? What is your response?

If ready, ask God to grow inside you the unique ways you can live your purpose during the days ahead. Record a prayer about this below or in a separate journal.

God continue to reveal to me your purpose in me. Thank you for your faithfulness. Keep the vision ahead the oars in the water, use all things to your glory.

TOGETHER AT THE TABLE
Group Session

Devotional Open
Open the group session by reading aloud the following quote. Invite a minute or two of response.

> "People are unreasonable, illogical and self-centered. Love them anyway. . . . If you are successful, you may win false friends and true enemies. Succeed anyway. The good you do today may be forgotten tomorrow. Do good anyway. Honesty and transparency make you vulnerable. Be honest and transparent anyway. What you spend years building may be destroyed overnight. Build anyway. People who really want help may attack you if you help them. Help them anyway. Give the world the best you have and you may get hurt. Give the world your best anyway."
>
> *Mother Teresa*

Read the passage below followed by an opening prayer asking God to be central and honored in the group today.

> "The Spirit of the Sovereign Lord is on me, because the Lord has anointed me to preach good news to the poor. He has sent me to bind up the brokenhearted, to proclaim freedom for the captives and release from darkness for the prisoners, to proclaim the year of the Lord's favor"
> (Isaiah 61:1, 2).

Review the At-Home Prep
Prepare for the discussion by spending a minute glancing through the thoughts you noted at home about Questions 1–3 on page 26.

Discussion
Begin the discussion by sharing your response to question 1 on page 26, prepared at home before the session.

When ready, continue your discussion by responding to the following quotes from *Soul Craving*.

WHAT'S THE PURPOSE?

"As Christians, what turns us on, motivates us, preoccupies us? Where is our best energy invested?

Look, for a moment, at the list below. On a scale of one through four, with one being most important and four being least important, how would you rank the items based on the time and energy Christians give to each?

> *Intimacy with God*
> *Behavior*
> *Serving others*
> *Beliefs"*

Soul Craving, p. 134

GRACE SPACE

Some groups hold one another accountable to certain beliefs and behaviors. Today, as we discuss our purpose and calling in Christ, we remember that we are first accountable to live by grace—to live life out of our calling and belovedness in Christ.

As a group, take a moment to rank the list as directed above. After that, rank them as you think God might. Why such a difference? On a personal level, what is one specific way you feel invited to live in God's priorities?

A NEW FOOD

"Many of us have had a lot of what the world has to offer, yet we are still hungry, restless, dissatisfied, puzzled. We wonder whether, perhaps, the solution is to get bigger helpings of what we have already had. But Jesus reveals an entirely new food. 'My food,' says Jesus, 'is to do the will of him who sent me and to finish his work.'

Our food, too, is to do the will of the one who put us here—to love, serve, and reconcile others to God according to our unique call. May we hunger for that food, find it, and be filled."

Soul Craving, p. 170

In what way might the unsatisfied cravings of your life be connected with a hunger to more deeply live your purpose and calling in God? What's attractive about pursuing your call? What feels hard or puzzling? How could this group help?

When ready, discuss question 2 on page 26.

GROUP BIBLE REFLECTION
JOSHUA 1:1-9—COURAGE FOR THE CALL

Ask a group member to read the passage aloud. Then spend about five minutes silently pondering the story, noticing whether a single word, phrase, or idea speaks to you. If so, what might God be inviting you toward through this?

> If the discussion becomes too theoretical, gently guide the focus back to God's personal word to each member through the text.

As you reflect on the passage and this whole lesson, what convictions about the future start to emerge in you? What is God's next step for you in your interests, vocation, relationships, passions, or other life areas?

Grace yourself! For some, a sense of God's calling is certain and exciting. For others it is vague, confusing, and even a little depressing. Allow yourself lots of grace to simply share your heart with the God who loves and delights in you exactly where you are.

Discussion
After the time of silent reflection above, share your responses with the group.

Toward the end of your discussion, share your answers to question 3 on page 26, prepared at home.

Closing Prayer
Allow the group leader to guide you in this closing prayer.

> ### Leader:
> *As you prayerfully think back over our time today, if there is one thought or idea that stands out as most important, what would it be? Might this be God speaking to you? Spend a moment prayerfully reflecting on this.* (pause)
>
> *If something has especially spoken to you today, what would you like to say to God about this? Silently share your heart with God for a moment.* (pause)

What, perhaps, would God like to say to you in return? (pause)

Finally, just relax in God's love and care for you. Invite God to plant his powerful Word deep inside you to grow and bear fruit in the days ahead. (pause)

Amen.

Take-Away Menu
4–5 Minute Take-Away Activity

LISTENING FOR GOD'S CALL

Every day we experience a vast variety of emotions. Our feelings register happiness, anxiety, anticipation, joy, dread, peace, anger, and a thousand variations on those themes. In recent years Christians have somewhat devalued our God-given emotions as unreliable in signaling to us important things to which we need to listen. Still, with balance, it's often

> FOR THE LEADER
> Look ahead now to the instructions for the special *Group Bible Reflection* activity for Session 5.

helpful to consciously pay attention to the specific experiences that make us happy or sad, joyful or despairing, full or empty.

A consistent sense of inner fullness or emptiness resulting from particular activities, relationships, and involvements may signal something God is calling us toward or cautioning us away from. We learn about God, ourselves, and our own unique calling by paying attention to the things in life that fill us up or make us empty.

Activity: Regularly ask yourself these questions:
♦ What activities and relationships filled me up today?
♦ What activities and relationships made me feel empty today?
♦ Is God saying anything in this? Is he calling me toward or away from anything?

Visit these questions daily, if possible. Do any patterns emerge over time? What might these patterns suggest about God's calling and guidance going forward? Write any insights you notice.

31

SATISFIED
PART 1

"IT HAS BEEN SAID, 'LET US GLANCE AT SIN, BUT GAZE AT CHRIST.' . . .
POWER FOR CHANGE, A WILLINGNESS TO RELEASE OLD COPING DEVICES,
AND THE INSPIRATION TO EMBRACE THE CROSS OF CHRIST IN THE WAY
OUR ILLS REQUIRE ARE MADE POSSIBLE BY A PERSONAL, GROWING VISION
OF JESUS CHRIST."

SOUL CRAVING, PP. 194, 195

SAMPLING THE FEAST
Preparing for the Group Session

Complete the following at home:
♦ Read chapters 13–15 in *Soul Craving*
♦ Ponder the Bible reflections on the next page
♦ Jot down some thoughts in response to questions 1–3

LEADER PREPARATION
In addition to the preparation on this page:
♦ release the session to God, expecting to experience his grace-filled activity
♦ prepare materials for the special *Group Bible Reflection* activity
♦ pray for the group members

---

1. Note one or two ideas that especially get your attention in the chapter readings and At-Home Bible Reflections for this session.

2. If you could distill to just one word what God is speaking to you as you reflect on the material, what would that word be? Why does this word emerge for you?

3. What is one practical way you will respond this week to God's call to you through the Bible reflections and readings?

Reflection 1

Genesis 22:1-18

In this passage the things that make yielding to God sometimes so hard are plainly shown—God's demands seem unreasonable, uncaring, and destined for a terrible end! Imagine Abraham and Isaac's journey to the altar. Where are you on your own journey to the land of the yielded?

He was listening obedient yielded

Possible ways to interact with this passage include:

Verse 2   What precious thing does intimacy with God require you to place on the altar right now? *The rest of the story; Money.*

Verse 6   What practical activities or attitudes today would represent yielding to God? *Listening obedience.*

Verses 15-18   What unexpected blessings might your yielded life bring to you and many others? *He had to look up The Lord will provide*

Isaac - questioning, obedient, trusting God.

Reflection 2

Lamentations 3:16-26

We often flee suffering as something empty of God, even as a sign of his displeasure. It takes great courage to relax in our suffering, to rest for a moment and listen for God's voice in the midst of it. Read the passage, listening for connections with your life. Then sit quietly in the presence of some physical, mental, or emotional situation that is causing you to suffer at this time. For five or ten minutes, pray these words from verses 24-26 of today's passage:

"I say to myself, 'The Lord is my portion; therefore I will wait for him.' The Lord is good to those whose hope is in him, to the one who seeks him; it is good to wait quietly for the salvation of the Lord."

Note your thoughts about this prayer time.

TOGETHER AT THE TABLE
Group Session

Devotional Open

Open the group session by reading aloud the following quote. Invite a minute or two of response.

> "Some people want to see God with their eyes as they see a cow, and to love Him as they love their cow—for the milk and cheese and profit it brings them. This is how it is with people who love God for the sake of outward wealth or inward comfort. They do not rightly love God, when they love Him for their own advantage. Indeed, I tell you the truth, any object you have in your mind, however good, will be a barrier between you and the inmost Truth."
>
> *Meister Eckhart*

response?

Read the passage below followed by an opening prayer asking God to be central and honored in the group today.

> "But whatever was to my profit I now consider loss for the sake of Christ. What is more, I consider everything a loss compared to the surpassing greatness of knowing Christ Jesus my Lord, for whose sake I have lost all things. I consider them rubbish, that I may gain Christ" (Philippians 3:7, 8).

pray.

Review the At-Home Prep

Prepare for the discussion by spending a minute glancing through the thoughts you noted at home about Questions 1–3 on page 32.

Discussion

Begin the discussion by sharing your response to question 1 on page 32, prepared at home before the session.

When ready, continue your discussion by responding to the following quotes from *Soul Craving*.

STRUGGLING WITH THE GIANT

"Victor Hugo, the great French novelist of the nineteenth century, was sitting in his study one sunny morning when he heard a tap-tap-tapping against the window. Rising to investigate he discovered a lone bee, trapped inside, flinging himself repeatedly against the glass in an attempt to get to the garden beyond. On the floor beneath the window lay a half-dozen dead bees that had pursued a similar strategy before running out of gas.

GRACE SPACE
Today's themes—transformation, surrender, and suffering— uncover some basic connections between us: we all struggle with God, we yearn for transformation, and we suffer and are in pain. May this group be a place today where we lovingly and safely probe these things together.

"Hugo lifted a napkin from a table and attempted to capture the bee to guide it out an open window. The bee frantically plunged this way and that in an attempt to escape. Eventually Hugo was able to gently grasp the frightened bee and slip it through the window. In a moment, the bee was floating freely about the garden."

Soul Craving, pp. 203, 204

Why did the bee struggle so hard against Hugo? Does this connect in any way with your struggling points at this moment with God?

UNEXPECTED SOLUTIONS

"We must become convinced of something that God has known for a very long time but we have not yet comprehended: 'My grace is sufficient for you, for my power is made perfect in weakness' (2 Corinthians 12:9). The helplessness provoked by suffering [and surrender] gets us there. It creates in us a weakness that eventually convinces us to lay aside our innumerable fruitless strategies in exchange for God's unexpected solutions."

Soul Craving, p. 232

What would be involved today in releasing your "innumerable fruitless strategies" into God's hands and yielding yourself into his solution? Will you go there?

When ready, discuss question 2 on page 32.

GROUP BIBLE REFLECTION
JOHN 12:20-28—UNEXPECTED FRUIT

Ask a group member to read the passage
aloud. Either do the optional activity or
spend about five minutes silently writing
your thoughts in response to the questions
below. As you reflect, recall that Jesus'
words in the passage are spoken in view of
his looming death.

What are Jesus' possible longings, hopes, or
fears at this time? What choices is he likely
making in his relationship with his Father?

> OPTIONAL ACTIVITY
> For today's *Group Bible
> Reflection*, provide a piece of
> modeling clay to each group
> member. Ask them to ponder
> the passage and questions, then
> to form the clay into a symbol
> that represents God's core
> message to them through the
> text. Allow about ten minutes
> for the personal reflection and
> clay molding. Encourage the
> groups to share with each other
> the meaning of their symbols.

How do Jesus' thoughts and feelings
connect with your own challenges in yielding your life to God? What
invitation do you find in Jesus' example or words?

Discussion
After the time of silent reflection above, share your responses with the group.

Toward the end of your discussion, share your answers to question 3 on
page 32, prepared at home.

Closing Prayer
Allow the group leader to guide you in this closing prayer.

Leader:
*As you prayerfully think back over our time today, if there is one thought
or idea that stands out as most important? Might this be God speaking to
you? Spend a moment prayerfully reflecting on this.* (pause)

*If something has especially spoken to you today, what would you like to
say to God about this? Silently share your heart with God for a moment.*
(pause)

What, perhaps, would God like to say to you in return? (pause)

Finally, just relax in God's love and care for you. Invite God to plant his powerful Word deep inside you to grow and bear fruit in the days ahead. (pause)

Amen.

Take-Away Menu
10 Second Take-Away Activity

CONTENTMENT & TRANSFORMATION

What happens when, in the midst of pressing life problems, we deliberately choose to content ourselves in God? Interesting things take place. We gradually become grounded and transformed by the reality that God himself is more important than a solution to our problems. And unexpectedly, this gives God room to become active in our lives in ways he wasn't before.

Activity: Notice one area of your life in which you desire God's transformation or rescue. From time to time during the day, by an act of your will, deliberately choose that you will be content in God in this area. Thank him that whether or not this area ever changes you will rest in his care for you. Thank him that despite appearances you are loved and everything is well in him.

Note: If the area you have in mind is very important to you and you have very definite preferences for how you'd like God to act, relaxing in God in this way may be hard. But if you choose to do so, you will honor God, aid in your own inner freedom, and give the Holy Spirit much elbow room to do surprising things in your life.

Mon: Nov 3rd 6 30/p

SATISFIED
PART 2

Satisfy

"OUR ABILITY TO REST IS ROOTED IN THE GOODNESS AND POWER OF GOD. THE FACT THAT GOD CARES, AND HAS THE POWER TO HELP US IN OUR PREDICAMENTS, MAKES IT SAFE FOR THE HUMAN HEART TO RELAX."

SOUL CRAVING, P. 242

SAMPLING THE FEAST
Preparing for the Group Session

Complete the following at home:
♦ Read chapters 16 and 17 in *Soul Craving*
♦ Ponder the Bible reflections on the next page
♦ Jot down some thoughts in response to questions 1–3

1. Note one or two ideas that especially get your attention in the chapter readings and At-Home Bible Reflections for this session.

> LEADER PREPARATION
> In addition to the preparation on this page:
> ♦ read this lesson beforehand, noting ideas that seem important for the discussion
> ♦ during the session, continually release the meeting to God, trusting he is present and active
> ♦ be aware of any final thoughts you'd like to share with the members as the group comes to a close

2. If you could distill to just one word what God is speaking to you as you reflect on the material, what would that word be? Why does this word emerge for you?

3. What is one practical way you will respond this week to God's call to you through the Bible reflections and readings?

AT-HOME BIBLE REFLECTIONS

Reflection 1
Mark 10:13-16
It is hard to overstate the impact that embracing our identity as God's dearly loved children has on enabling us to live a life of relaxed trust. Imagine the characters of this passage, their thoughts, desires, goals, and fears. Then consider the following:

◆ Why are the children able to receive and experience Jesus' blessing? What inner attitudes come naturally to these children?

> to come to them   trust.
>
> to recieve from them   distractions

◆ What habits or attitudes lead the disciples to obstruct blessing?

> don't touch Jesus.

◆ Put yourself in the scene. What is Jesus' desire toward you? How might you live beneath his loving touch from moment to moment?

Reflection 2
Matthew 14:22-33
In this powerful passage Peter leaves the security of his boat in response to Jesus' call. In books and sermons poor Peter usually gets a bad rap for soon sinking under the frightening waves. But the courage and trust of Peter's first few steps is impressive.

What does Peter teach you about responding to God in your life right now? Ask: "What personal boat am I being invited to step out of in response to Jesus' call?" Write down God's word to you through the passage.

> take courage.   just do it
>
> don't be afraid   step out.

> God will be there to save me.

TOGETHER AT THE TABLE
Group Session

Devotional Open

As you open the group session by reading aloud the following quote, reflect on God's invitation to rest our hearts entirely in him. Invite comments.

> "An old woman struggled along an uneven path toward home, a huge load of firewood balanced on her stooped shoulder. A passing wagon stopped. The driver offered the woman a ride to ease her journey. With gratefulness the woman painfully climbed aboard the back of the wagon, which once again began its way along the path. After some time the driver was surprised to notice that his passenger had not taken the heavy load of wood from her shoulder. 'Madame,' he exclaimed, 'surely you would be more comfortable if you rested your load on the wagon.' 'Oh, no!' answered the old woman. 'Thank you, but I wouldn't want to burden you further.'"

Read the passage below twice with a brief pause between for worship.

> "Listen to me, O house of Jacob, . . . you whom I have upheld since you were conceived, and have carried since your birth. Even to your old age and gray hairs I am he, I am he who will sustain you. I have made you and I will carry you; I will sustain you and I will rescue you" (Isaiah 46:3, 4).

Review the At-Home Prep

Prepare for the discussion by spending a minute glancing through the thoughts you noted at home about Questions 1–3 on page 38.

Discussion

Begin the discussion by sharing your response to question 1 on page 38, prepared at home before the session.

When ready, continue your discussion by responding to the following quotes from *Soul Craving.*

TASTING REST

"I wondered, What if that's true?
What if God actually cares about me
and has the power to help me? What
if I'm allowed to relax, to rest, to trust
in his love and mercy? What if it's OK
to quit this never-ending struggle to
perform for God and others, to justify
my existence by what I produce? . . .
For someone who is by nature a
Type A, whose inclination is always
to be on task, and whose social and religious conditioning has been to find
personal worth through the quantity and quality of what I produce, to taste
the rest of God is a revelation."

GRACE SPACE

**In this final session, our themes—
rest and responsiveness—tap into
our appetite for a life of relaxed
and courageous trust in God.
God's goodness and power make
it safe to risk such a life. During
this session may we help each
other move forward toward the
trust our souls crave.**

Soul Craving, pp. 240–242

What would it mean to you to rest in Christ? In what way would you like to
rest your life in God right now? What makes this hard? What is one baby step
forward?

UNEXPECTED SOLUTIONS

"'Stand firm and you will see the deliverance the Lord will bring you today'
(Exodus 14:13). . . . That is God's reason for obedience. . . . So God pushes
us into corners. He erects huge walls before us. He hems us in and squeezes
away our options until there is nothing left for us to do but flee or trust.
Mutiny or obey. Revolt or rely on him. If we risk responding, we find ourselves
taking part in God's supernatural solution to our dilemma. And here is the
key: as we become caught up in the swirl of this activity, we become changed.
It is as though in the process of transforming the situation, God's miracle
filters through us, transforming us as well!"

Soul Craving, p. 271

Tell the group about a difficult time when you responded obediently to God.
What was the result? What part of you needed to die in order to respond?
What part of you came alive?

When ready, discuss question 2 on page 38.

GROUP BIBLE REFLECTION
GENESIS 12:1-4; HEBREWS 11:8—TRAVELING ON

Ask a group member to read both passages aloud. Then spend about five minutes silently reflecting and writing down thoughts in response to the passages and the questions below.

> FOR THE LEADER
> During this final *Group Bible Reflection*, encourage the members to think about the passages as they relate to their vocation, family life, volunteer activities, and general life with God in the days ahead.

What are you hungry for next in your life with God? What does Abraham's example call you toward in your vocation, family life, volunteer activities, and general life with God?

What habits, assumptions, and perhaps untruths do you need to leave behind in order to go to the "land" God is showing you?

Discussion
After the time of silent reflection above, share your responses with the group.

Toward the end of your discussion, share your answers to question 3 on page 38, prepared at home.

Closing Prayer
Allow the group leader to guide you in this closing prayer.

> *Leader:*
> *As you prayerfully think back over our time today, what one thought or idea stands out as most important? Might this be God speaking to you? Spend a moment prayerfully reflecting on this.* (pause)
>
> *If something has especially spoken to you today, what would you like to say to God about this? Silently share your heart with God for a moment.* (pause)
>
> *What, perhaps, would God like to say to you in return?* (pause)

Finally, just relax in God's love and care for you. Invite God to plant his powerful Word deep inside you to grow and bear fruit in the days ahead. (pause)

Amen.

Take-Away Menu
A Menu for the Future

"Discipline is remembering what we want."

Michael Dash

Your *Soul Craving* group experience has ended! So what's next? What activities and relationships below is God calling you toward that will help you continue to satisfy your heart in Jesus Christ?

♦ INTIMATE RELATIONSHIP. God encountered in:
> *Bible meditation and study, prayer, devotional reading, music, small group involvement, spiritual friendships, community worship, the arts, and more*

♦ INTEGRATED RELATIONSHIP. God woven throughout my:
> *Family, time, job, leisure, service, money, outreach, community, church, and more*

While every area above is important, as you consider moving into the months ahead, "listen" for the activities and relationships that God is especially calling you to embrace right now. What opportunities is he giving you to do that? If helpful, write down your thoughts to clarify your sense of guidance. As direction emerges, take practical steps to live out the things God is offering you.

BE CONNECTED! Finally, you are not built to live this life with God alone! Above all other things, stay connected in small groups with hungry people who have chosen to spend their lives nourishing their hearts in Jesus Christ. That's where the banquet is.

JOURNALING

JOURNALING

JOURNALING

JOURNALING